Christm

Twelve Poems for Rosy Cheeks

ex libris

Candlestick Press

Published by:
Candlestick Press,
Diversity House, 72 Nottingham Road, Arnold, Nottingham NG5 6LF
www.candlestickpress.co.uk

Design and typesetting by Craig Twigg

Printed by Bayliss Printing Company Ltd of Worksop, UK

Cover illustration © Jenny Hancock
https://www.jennyhancockartist.co.uk/

Candlestick Press monogram © Barbara Shaw, 2008

© Candlestick Press, 2023

ISBN 978 1 913627 14 0

Acknowledgements

Thanks are due to the authors listed below for kind permission to use their poems,
all of which are published here for the first time:

Bill Adair, Valerie Bence, Jane Burn, Martyn Crucefix, Kerry Darbishire,
Marie-Louise Eyres, Annie Kissack, Aoife Mannix, Charlotte Oliver, Penny
Sharman, Giles Watson and Miriam Wei Wei Lo.

Contents   Page

A low owl at Christmas

I once walked up the lane with my children
by moonlit snow, power lines down – in the deepest dark
they had ever known; we made a small hand-held line,
six small feet and mine as we wended and crunched
up and down the small hill making tracks towards home.
Mitten muffled we kris-kringled our way
breath watching and laughing with dancing candles.
At the gate, and close to tick and warmth
in the all-embracing snow-silence   we turn as one
and with four sharp 'Oos' of icy breath –
a low owl leaps into freezing air
whispers his take-off to the Christmas moon

I play it like a silent film,
how this moonlight memory ties us like a knot.

Valerie Bence

The Snow, the Path, the Moon, the Leaf

"...upon the top of the tree—the sole remaining leaf..." Dorothy Wordsworth

Shall we imagine this copse is a ruined church? Each chiselled sharp
is snowed soft, each bough weighed gently down. Dorothy, as I walked
to meet you here I was a little afraid of the night — afraid of slipping,
of imagined wolves, of becoming lost; of blemishing such perfection
with my tread. I thought of you, and that though made me strong —
Dorothy, you would have gladly left your hearth to be part of this cold,
curious world. You would have tilted your head, noted every little thing
between land and sky. You would have loved the glitter of frost
in a tyre's tread, the flakes that wheeled around my head, the way
they mingled with stars. The space above me seemed alive with flight.
I passed my favourite house — its sandy-rough eroded stones
were flurry skinned, its homely casements glowed. The scent of hay
carried from the barn nearby. If I peeped in, I almost believed I'd see you,
diary wide as a window, inking memories out. The cars along the street
were stilled with drifts, half-buried like hardy cattle weathering it out.
I placed my boots with slow care — as I pressed them to the ground
the snow gave out a song. It sang me along to the way through
the wood, where I knew you'd be waiting. Dorothy, look how the moon
has dosed the dark's throat — a mithridate, sweet to the taste —
how tame a shadow's threat is made beneath its light! Listen, my dear,
to the plainchant wind. You would have written, as I do now,
about the beauty of this place. We have offered our words to the pale
field of the page. Every trace of your feet has been wintered away,
yet I know exactly where you have been. You point out a leaf — the last
of its kind clinging to a tree. Our mouths shape smiles. Tomorrow
is Christmas day. Dorothy, our gifts have come early and Nature
has wrapped them in white. Our breath twines and I am so glad
you are here. I show you angels of distant smoke.
Not every ghost is someone we must fear.

Jane Burn

Intimate Pavements

Gone seven o'clock on Christmas Eve,
And I take my memory for a walk
Round the village where I was weaned and green.
It should be snowing.

This is the house of my granny's Christmas shortbread.
The walls look the same, but different windows
Have allowed my memories to scatter.
New family. New recipes.

The hopeful letters I wrote to Santa Claus
Were posted up that crumbling chimney stack,
Bound for the North Pole, postage paid.
Bedtime at fever pitch.

Christmas morning, and the streets buzzed with kids,
Evicted while the kitchen exploded.
Cowboys. Nurses. Footballs. Dolls' prams.
All the gender stereotypes.

I pass the bus-stop where I had my first kiss,
The taste of perfume, sweet as Christmas itself,
Only to be dumped on New Year's Eve.
Painful as holly jags.

Now I walk where my existence began,
A place of intimate pavements,
Where I yearn to hear the peal of steeple bells,
Their carefree hullabaloo.

If I feel I belong anywhere,
It is here, drawn in and properly placed,
Under a dark-bright Christmas sky,
Between ghosts and guardian angels.

Bill Adair

Winter Gathering

Here we go gathering sticks and stems,
endless fronds in frozen hands.
Here we go gathering half the lane
on a cold and frosty morning.

Hazel and hawthorn (bring secateurs),
willow and holly (leave berries for birds),
a rabble of burdock, wild carrot, knapweed,
pine cones and teasel heads emptied of seed.

Deck the halls! Fa la la! Back we are staggering,
ivy is swaggering, here comes the gathering,
brownery, greenery strutting their finery,
up in the gallery minstrels play:

Down in the deepwood, I saw a fair maiden.
her mantle was grey and her manner was wild.
I stepped up beside her but she turned her back on me
and spoke not one word for she was winter's child.

And we had gathered sticks and stems,
endless fronds in frozen hands.
We had gathered half the lane
and brought the winter home.

Annie Kissack

Boxing Day walk when Lili loved us all, 2001.

We could see for miles across the Tame Valley.
It was hard ice and snow piled high on the banks.
Mark, Lili and me had red noses and cheeks.
We were happy, amazed by patterns of ice in puddles.
We laughed when we smashed them with our feet.
The sun came out and warmed our hearts, tips
of fingers defrosted. We knew nothing of what
was to come. How a girl's identity can change:
fast as a speed train, an avalanche to break
the strongest minds. We knew nothing of the pain
of separation, when she blamed her dad for everything,
shaved her head, chose another name. I look at the photos
from that walk, a merry time to keep tight to my chest,
know that we walked in ice and snow, smiled in sunshine,
reached the White Hart Inn, ate golden crisps, drank pop
and mulled wine, heard carols blasting out of speakers,
Hark the Herald Angel Sing, in The Bleak Midwinter.

Penny Sharman

Christmas Walk - A Snow Cento

There was no more snow during the night,
frost on the great bay-window spawns snow and pink roses,
the wind blows Niagara rainbows of snow over the city
where they wear galoshes to their armpits all year-round.
It lays in ditches and in hollows, one vast shell.

Upon the hard crest of a snowdrift we tread, heads tossed
back in song, and on ripe lips catch the perfect flakes.
Sunlight is too gold, the snow half gracious,
fruitful, silver-quick, looping air like birds to broken bones,
knotting rags of it on the limbs of trees. To look at the snow

too long has a hypnotic effect, cold seems to cramp the bones,
candles have to be lit, ice in the jugs smashed. The long sword
of the frozen river shines. There's a slight silver chink
of your spurs. And after dark, elms all apple bloom
at the backs of houses where light shows around the edges of curtains.

Marie-Louise Eyres

Lines from the following texts: Philip Larkin's *A Girl in Winter* and poems titled
Snow by Louis Macneice, Hardie St.Martin, Anna Akhmatova and Paul Petrie.

Walk With Me in December

through the forest of Christmas trees
with their eyes twinkling on a dark afternoon.
The last of the light strewn tinsel
along the horizon. The air
pine needles in our lungs
as I take your hand, reminding myself
this is not illegal. We are allowed
to step out across the frozen fields.
The flash of robin brave in scarlet flames.

It has been a difficult year.
Expensive, wrapped in barbed wire,
the taste of coal in my mouth.
A small boy with his questions
I don't know how to answer.
But now the trees are snapping
their broken fingers to the hymn
of hallelujah. The imprint of your boot
cracking thin ice, muddy water
rushing through the cracks.
Your laughter a ribbon flowing
all the way to the North Pole.

Aoife Mannix

Fleecy Disney Christmas snowflakes

falling
so the street quiet was even more muffled
close to silence but for the creak of boots
my own and my son's and he was recounting
his numbers (as men often do—as I
did many times with my own father too)
the work numbers he'd posted that month
despite lockdown and how his new boss
was shaping up 'better than expected'

and all the while we walked he gathered
above his high strong brow like a jutting roof
a little shelf of snow on the dark fringe
he'd been compelled to grow (the barber
on the Broadway out of action for weeks)
and we agreed he'd come and get it fixed

so he'd bought and brought electric clippers
and back home we passed through the house
to the back garden—a black garden chair
set out under the snowfall—and there
I drove a firm plough up and over his scalp
through thick young dark hair that fell
in great clumps over the deepening snow
to lie like the darkest of brushstrokes
and after ten minutes you could imagine

the foxes had returned the previous night
for larger prey and had torn it to pieces
then we were done—both now shivering—
back through the warm house and perhaps
a quick complicit grin went between us
though unseen behind our baby-blue masks

Martyn Crucefix

Christmas Landscape

Wrapped in kitchen warmth
I stride out taking it with me
over fields under hedges,
all pigment erased, burnt umber
buried beneath a palette of tinsel-white.
Only the flame of a robin in a hawthorn
singing like a distant bell
catches the still air.

Across the valley sheep huddle
around bales of last summer, breath
rising like ancient signals: clover, vetch,
yellow rattle. I crunch on.
You show me how a winter sky glows
raw sienna against drifts, the name
of each tone: Payne's grey, indigo, flake white,
and how pines and holly by the river folded in ice

is worked with a palette knife.
You lay out the deep language of rabbit, fox
and hare dashed across a hungry canvas,
signatures stamped in flourishes of twos
and threes. By Judy's gate
I press an apple into Joey's soft muzzle
then double back, your hand in mine
brushed with snow.

Kerry Darbishire

Quick Trip to the Beach Before the Early Service
(Perth/Boorloo, Australia)

Seven fifteen. The sand is white as snow.
Our dog shoots up to the top of the dune
and turns, *Are you coming?* she asks *How soon?*
The question wags its tail. How do we know?
Are you coming? To take this day with us,
to crest the dune, to rush into the water?
Running, one foot sinks in, then the other.
Soft sand before the hard. Small waves discuss
arrivals. Ours and yours. What will it mean
to sing of your coming? *Noel, Noel.*
We crowd the pews. We wait. We feast. We spell
your name in fairy lights, like a wish, like a dream
of God-with-us: you have come, you are coming, you come
breaking the water, burning like summer sun.

Miriam Wei Wei Lo

The Caldon Canal

Where I grew up the sun was too fierce
on my skin for much by way of walking.
We whiled away the Yuletide huddled
not around a fireplace but the cooler -
and the season's harbingers were bronze
plump bombs of Christmas beetles
champing on *Eucalyptus*. But then one year
when I was eleven there was December
in Longsdon where my grandmother
hung out suet for bluetits under icicled
eaves - the snug-carpeted staircase wreathed
with Grandad's cherry pipesmoke - and filigrees
of frost-flowers formed on pantry windows.

That first morning I stepped wide-eyed
out into the whitebreathed world
and skittered down the lane - Wellington-deep
in snow - past the skeletons of umbels
frosted with cows' breath - down to where
a stone bridge spanned the Caldon Canal
frozen solid and snaking under snowdrifts.
Holly-coloured barges were bound by ice -
their chimneys emitting thin spindles
of woodsmoke - white and apple-scented.

Off in a spinney, a woodpecker rattled.
I knelt down - prodded the surface
with a stick - tested half my weight -
then stepped out muffled and exultant
onto the frozen water

and heard the awl-bird's yaffle
worshipping the cold.

Giles Watson

Unboxed

Baubled by over-indulgence, the crowd's pace
along the prom is slow; on two feet, four
or shiny wheels, we move through magnified light.

Some step with the joy of those newly-socked
or under hats and scarves still happily paired
for now. Focus freed from yesterday's four walls

to boundless blue extravagantly
stretched in all directions. Safe within
the snow-globe gift of Christmas, I do not

scan the offing for a stormy portent
nor let thoughts drift as far as new year's tides
but delight in now, this buffet of sights:

enthusiastic dogs in jumpers, glad
loved ones and merry toddlers plump as puddings,
all fairy-lit by sunshine-glittered sea.

Charlotte Oliver